Routine Heaven

Jack Myers

Texas Review Press
Huntsville, Texas

Copyright © 2005 by Jack Myers
All rights reserved
Printed in the United States of America

FIRST EDITION, 2005

Requests for permission to reproduce material from this work should be sent to:

>Permissions
>*Texas Review* Press
>English Department
>Sam Houston State University
>Huntsville, TX 77341-2146

Acknowledgments

The author wishes to thank the following publications for the first appearance of some of the poems in this book:

The American Poetry Review, The Café Review, Crazy Horse, Crying Sky, Espejo, Poetry, Smartish Pace, TriQuarterly

New poems from *The Glowing River: New and Selected Poems*: "Parable of the Burden," "Whatever You Do," "Life Boat," "Mindfulness," "Pets," "The Tao of Light," "The Flicker," "Building the Temple," "Untitled," "Now," "The Sequin," "Incarnation," "On Purpose," "Alchemy," "The Never-Mind Life," "She Didn't Know and He Never Said," "Smoke Break," "Eyelash on a Piece of Jade," "The Great Work," "The Deep Blue Sea of Surrender," "The Iridescent Flashings of the Integral One," "Catching the Hummingbird," "Star Trek," and "Hanging Branches" were originally published by Invisible Cities Press, Montpelier, 2001.

Cover art: *A Place in the Sun*, by Billy Hassell
Photograph of Jack Myers: Courtesy of The Writer's Garret
Cover design by Paul Ruffin

Library of Congress Cataloging-in-Publication Data
Myers, Jack Elliott, 1941-
 Routine heaven / Jack Myers.-- 1st ed.
  p. cm.
 ISBN 1-881515-78-8 (alk. paper)
 I. Title.
PS3563.Y42R68 2005
813'.54--dc22

2005013924

FOR THEA

home within my home

"Why, from a stone I can carve either a warrior or a priest. It merely depends on the flaws."
—Ven Bergamudre

"If I didn't like the perfume of dead flowers, I couldn't plant seeds of joy."
—Paula Goldman

Contents

Worry Wart, Run Away, Never Wake Up

Pets	2
The Never-Mind Life	3
Escape	4
Eyelash on a Piece of Jade	5
An Old Dog's Tale	6
Strip Polka	7
Sweat	8
She Didn't Know and He Never Said	9
Bypass	10
Conspicuous by My Absence	11
What Is All Center and Has No Edges?	12
The Tea of Paradise	13

On Earth As It Is in Heaven

Life Boat	16
Pinch	17
On Earth As It Is in Heaven	18
Smoke Break	19
Building the Temple	20
Builder's Soil	21
Alchemy	22
He Does This Instead	23
"Blah, blah, blah, blah, Jackie"	24
The Sequin	25
Fiction Theories	26
The Achievement Test	27
Belief	28
Picturing Happiness	29

The Great Work

The Great Work	32
Star Trek	34
Parable of the Burden	35
Routine	36
Heaven	37
Living Large	38
The "I Used To Be (Blank) But Now I Am (Blank) Exercise"	40
Writing on Not Writing	41
While Reading the Work of Another Poet	42
Woodpecker Event Horizon	43
The Rest of Me	44

The Failed Calligrapher	45
Not the Work, Not the Life	46
Sweet Dreams	47
How Do You Like My Hair?	48
Ashville	49

The Wisdom of the Idiots

Indebted	52
Unless	53
When I Heard My Name Being Called	54
Blue Skies	55
Whatever You Do	56
Vacancy	57
Mindfulness	58
On Purpose	59
The Deep Blue Sea of Surrender	60
The Iridescent Flashings of The Integral One	61
The Wisdom of the Idiots	62
Curriculum Vitae	63
Hanging Branches	64
Inside Out	65
Catching the Hummingbird	66
Pouring Water Downhill	67

Unconditional Surrender

The Flicker	70
Now	71
Doorway	72
The Tao of Light	73
Continuity Drives Through the Division of Things	74
Prescience	75
Me	76
Who, What, When, Where, and Why	77
Incarnation	78
The New Gods	79
Live As If You Were Dead	80
Track Record	81
Unconditional Surrender	82
Fragments	83
You Will Live a Very Long Time . . . *in bed*	84
All the Power That Has Ever Existed Is Here Now	85
Sea Level	86

Worry Wart, Run Away, Never Wake Up

Pets

My three dogs follow me wherever I go.
I should name them for my hungers:
Worry Wart, Run Away, Never Wake Up,

call them *There's no place like home*,
Life is beautiful and precious,
and *What will be will be*.

But that's what I was told by my parents
when I hungered, as if they were Chinese fishermen
tying nooses around the cormorants they kept.

Now I pay tribute to my hungers,
knock down the fence to honor breaking out,
let sleeping dogs lie to protest the indignities of living;

I go outside and come back in over and over
so the clichés that contained them
are the freedoms I contain. But better yet,
my dogs are just my dogs again.

The Never-Mind Life

After dropping a tranquilizer on the rug,
which coated it with hair and dust,

I blew it off and, instead of taking it,
I put it back in the jar and shook it twice.

This way I made sure I'd never know
when I'd choose the dirty one again.

Or, now maybe all of them would be tainted
the way everything tastes after brushing your teeth.

Or, possibly, having jostled it around with the others,
the pill would somehow clean itself.

It wasn't what you'd call a life-threatening situation,
but from now on the whole pill-taking thing would get complex.

Escape

I nailed that wire mesh against the bottom of the fence
to stop my dog from tunneling under it,
because, once out, we thought, he'd never come back,
which, come to think of it, is how he came to us.

Weeds have grown up through the mesh and that thing
in my dog that kept wanting to start another life
is as old as the mesh that's now so rusted it's become part
    of the fence.

Do I even need the fence now that my dog is such a friend?
But every time I pass the mesh and for an instant
I don't know what it is--this rusted thing I rolled up
and crushed down flat with dead grass trapped inside it—
I make a mental note, Get rid of it.

Eyelash on a Piece of Jade

After 5,000 years
one would think
that Asian artists
would lose interest in painting
a white lotus
floating on a pond
beneath a distant mountain peak

as if to say only stillness
can capture the quickest blink
of that maiden crying in the foreground,
lying in a bamboo thicket
blown down and spreading out
from the long black sigh of her hair,

as if to paint the paradox of art:
"What's eternal is what will not last."

I travel back to before my birth
to the lust my father felt
for my mother in Hokku province, 1941,
after he surprised her
with a piece of rare green jade
she left to my wife
who took it off last night
after we argued and decided to just stay home
on our weekly special night out
we promised always to reserve just for us.

An Old Dog's Tale

My dog's tail
exactly touches the floor.

How perfect nature is!
How mathematical!

Or maybe the floor
keeps rubbing her fur away.

Last night in a dream
my son came to me to be comforted.

He must've been the part of me that needed help.
But I couldn't shake the feeling that my real son needed me.

Like when the missiles rained down on Baghdad and Kabul,
the women there turned out to be very beautiful.

On the other hand, my dog's legs also touch the floor.

Strip Polka

You said I always lose our bets
because you only bet on a sure thing.
So what do you think possessed me
to bet you if I could stop smoking
then I could do anything I want with you
and if I couldn't stop smoking, then
you could do anything you want to me?

Sweat

My dogs like to pull me around the block,
mailbox by mailbox. Their sense of smell
is so superior to mine that I have to brag to them
my brain's so big, I'm just taking it for a walk.

They get a whiff of the Mexican river-mud and sweat
rising out of the bricks, the salt breeze off the Japanese metal,
the rich smell of jungle rot from mahogany, the Asian jasmine
and Malaysian tires, the Portland cement and Chinese bolts.

They can sniff what dog's in love with what dog isn't
the way the fly on the lip of my beer glass smells its way back
to a sweaty horse in Dusseldorf outside a German brewery.

Ah, it's good to be the Alpha of the pack, Odysseus lashed by
dead-reckoning to temptation and terror: lonely housewives
in empty MacMansions, automatic sprinklers spraying oblivion
over this subdivision sailing, by God, by dog, by nose, by heart.

She Didn't Know and He Never Said

She didn't know he planted marigolds outside their window
any more than he could see the flowers she dreamed of
    while he slept,

or that when she took a shower, which is how she spoke,
by saying everything at once, he made it a point never to
    flush the toilet;

how he withstood the daily firing squad of bored students
who, like the x-mas gifts she bought year-round and hid
    in her closet, he kept unconscious.

He was reared to show his love like the starving octopus who
ate itself up, arm after arm after arm, then its head until it
    was an undying presence

turned inside-out in a corner of its murky aquarium, living
off the sadness inside the little things he never said and
    she never noticed,

which through hard work held them together and came to
assume a life of its own, which made their lives seem more
    mysterious, a little better.

Bypass

—for heart surgeon Baron Hamman

When everyone said they'd pray for me
I figured I'd feel a mild electrical shock
like when I used to lick 9-volt batteries.

Well, it turns out the sign God sent was nausea and a nagging
wife, like when I discovered the Holy Grail was a slumped-
over ashtray my daughter made at summer camp.

But I couldn't tell whether my life was actually saved or
    not.

So when people say *You're lucky to be alive* they seem like
my dog barking at the door at no one.
                        Oh, yes, I'm thankful to be alive,

but I'm embarrassed to admit that what's important to me
is not so much whether what happened was actually a
    matter of life and death,
it's whether what happened in the way it did was special
    or not.

Conspicuous by My Absence

The new students look up to me
as I introduce myself as the one
who'll show them what they'll write
will not be what they meant.

One girl's missing.
So's the part of me that smoked
to get out of feeling locked inside my head.

"Is Allison Strausberg here?" I ask,

and everyone's attention is galvanized
into a white space as large as the room
called Allison.

I think I should say something
that'll make me feel real to the students—
like all the things I've never said.

*Ok, I was the Captain of the Tumbling Team
who couldn't do a flip. And to tell the truth
when I write I don't know where I'm going,
but I'm on a roll at the edge of confessing
it's impossible to teach what truly matters.
But I can show the heart is a desert
so there's a place where we can thirst.*

That'd be way too much
though it's what I meant.
I suppose we're better off,
my caravanning band of little nomads and I,
crossing the desert in search of what I always say
which is in search of what I meant.

What Is All Center and Has No Edges?

Trying to find the origins of anger
by looking into my heart
is like a dead leaf feeling for its roots.

My dog barks, voicing his desire
to make contact, to attach.

My desire is to erase the space
between here and the tree
while fiercely resisting that.

My dog crooks his head and looks at me,
his human master from whom all good things come,
as if to say "Why can't you just enjoy that?"

The Tea of Paradise

Like the Oleander which I dug up
though it was lush and gorgeous and difficult to destroy,
my most beautiful daydreams have always been poisonous.

A mere tea brewed from its paradisiacal flowers
can trigger heart failure.
I've always wanted to blossom inside the exotic,

not live like those who pass through each other
on the way to each other,
but live without knowing it.

Not live without knowing it
wishing I could live without knowing it.

Anyway, everyone kept insisting I get rid of it.
But it was so beautiful, and dangerous
only if you ate it. I guess it stood for me as proof
that I was living extravagantly someplace else.

On Earth As It Is in Heaven

Life Boat

There's been a lot of fighting
in this little boat
though I've been alone
as before I was born.

I've split the gunnels,
widened the cracks,
and the stern is pulling away.

That's why I'm afraid
of putting out to sea
with or without it,

still bickering about how
my little journey
still stuck in sand
should and shouldn't be.

Pinch

Why do I try so hard to know
what can't be known?

If there's nothing beyond this life
then I won't know it then either.

And if I happen to get soaked up in the omnivorating oneness
then I won't know it then either.

Even if my karma comes and transforms me
it'll all be the same, only different.

Better to bite into this half-ripened apple
and remember where I am.

On Earth As it Is in Heaven

I built a ladder
in the sky
out of my life.

But when I got to the top
there was nowhere to step off.

I never thought I'd end up
being what I built.

I thought I'd leave the ladder behind
like footprints in the snow that suddenly stop.

The idea being, when I was done,
others could use it.

I started shouting down to the others
"It's no use!"

when whatever happened next—
my pride in getting lost
or the feathery night moth
who landed in the garage door's electric eye
and miraculously held it up—
whatever happened, it was a rung, a step,
a handhold, a life.

Smoke Break

The students walk by me, their destinies
morphed into faces like homework
on how the journey's been so far.

I seem to be invisible to them. Like most things are
to them, I must look like what I am in the world.

But it's the best way to see the ambition and lust
and wreckage of mistakes splashed down like blossoms
from a dirt storm into a road.

When I was young and one of them, everyone's face
seemed alien. Now they look like friends. I want to shout help
and encouragement, give piggybacks away to happiness.

But I could use a little help to bid the last proud bit of me
good riddance: Selenia Rosario Colon, when I drove by your
orphanage that huge thing at the end of glory, which is
     humility,

passed through me like the wind these struggling faces
     leave behind,
the irreducible and most stubborn part of me that I can't
     surrender to,
the little voice that asked if we could stop and help.

Building the Temple

I would like to build a temple
out of stone by the sea.

A place to meditate and practice
harnessing the power of surrender.

But I can't carve or sculpt.

If I looked as long as it would take to learn to sculpt,
I could find the rocks that fit,

rocks whose religious faces pouring over them
surpassed art, whose imaginings were as difficult as carving.

But having faith the rocks are there and fit
whatever I imagine, is, in a way, building the temple.

Builder's Soil

When I built my dream home
and didn't replace the builder's soil with loam,
the petals on my roses fell away like childhood wishes.

But when I planted desert dwarfs and sages
in honor of burning through my prime,
they threw out such red and purple hallelujahs
it looked like wildfire climbing up a gasoline rain.

That's when I felt the destructive streak in me again
put its itchy finger on alchemy's glistening trigger.

Alchemy

My neighbor's trying to start his truck.
It coughs and sputters and backfires several times
before it finally starts up. The sound of it

says he's financially strapped yet considerate
so early in the morning in the way he soothes
and brushes the gas to a quiet idle,

as if some sweet old messages
from his penniless past are harbingers
of what will come next.

He thinks if he can get the truck to just turn over
he'll get one more day to start. My work is to
sit and see what's next.

How could I ever explain to him my work
is to become my neighbor, and then
while still in my pajamas looking like me sitting here,
become his truck?

He Does This Instead

Smoking a cigarette,
sipping black coffee,
watching the sun rise,
I pretend I'm dead
so I can feel the black seam
between living inside and outside
feel itself up.

Then I subtract that
so I can feel my life
as I am living it—
sunlight and human smoke—
and calculate my great subtraction
down to a pure hum of human being
that assumes the shape of normal feeling and thought,
like making love or calling up my children

before the trillion miniature suns
in each transparent cell of my body
light up and blind me by my living,
before need backlights everything
and overwhelms knowing
that whatever it was, whatever I did,
it was one of the great pleasures.

"Blah, blah, blah, blah, Jackie"

I've followed my heart
the way my dog's followed me,
knowing only a command or two.

But trying to decipher my heart
with my heart is equivalent to the way
all my knowledge ever did for me
was overpower me with thought.

Like the tongue, the brain, and the cock,
it says all things are just one thing
that opens onto everything,
and everything, dear heart, is about want.

The Sequin

What have I been waiting for?
For some science-fiction future
when I'll be able to beam myself down anywhere at will?

I'm like an awe-struck child in his parents' wardrobe,
feeling powerless because their sparkling garments of desire
come through louder and clearer than they do.

It's about being anything other than who I am, isn't it?

I'm a sunbeam shot from the sun
at a sequin on my mother's dress
whose purpose is to cover her body
by catching the light. To glamorize
and dazzle the eye and stir desire for another,
for something other than all this.
Toward what purpose?

Fiction Theories

One says if you know your character deeply enough
and write "Poor Gloria" those words would be suffused
with the weight of what you haven't said.

Another says just start with "Poor Gloria"
and then try to discover why she's dead.

Meanwhile, dear Reader, Gloria lives
in the margins of your imagination, as you do
in hers, feeling completely misunderstood.
Whether others know of her or not or think
she is or isn't real has nothing to do with it.

The Achievement Test

In my dream
I'm taking an achievement test
with my students.
But I'm not doing well.
Although it's multiple choice—
yes, no, none of the above—
all my answers feel ambiguous.

The proctor marches up to me and says
you don't have to take this test,
you're the teacher.

I run outside. I'm the teacher!
and wake relieved to be in real life.

I look up outside. There's the sun
drifting above the clouds like a pale moon,
like a half-wrong answer.

I don't know how to stop this test.

Belief

When I was young and believed in the power
of flying and being invisible and impervious
to everything because I was visible,
I practiced seeing through everything
so I could grasp whatever was beyond my reach.

I traded all that in for the power of giving up
and leaving and forgetting everything
so I could be emptied out like hunger
so that whatever was going to happen next
could happen next.

It wasn't living on the dark side of my defeats,
perfecting longing into a kind of desultory speech,
that dumbed me down small and hard enough
to meet the hardness of life. It was giving up
that taught me that belief is just the shadow side of leaving
without the leaving.

But I'm more like a rock climber now
who, as he's falling from a cliff,
though he believed the one bad move he was about to make
would probably be a mistake, went ahead and made it anyway,
because now I believe that being here and being anything,
even a man falling to his death,
is more powerful than belief.

Picturing Happiness

I am cultivating happiness
the way I nurtured grief.
Same full-page color spread
of a tropical flower,
only in black because
I only remember negatives,
spreading out like a prayer
against the same sky of constant care
I lavished on my grief. It'll have to have
the same suffocating atmosphere
imported from where I've been, but
it'll open slowly, almost sexually, in full color,
surrendering to what's rising through its cut green stem.

The Great Work

The Great Work

> *Then Dr. Bluespire...whispered into [the ape's] ear:*
> *"You look like a god sitting there.*
> *Why don't you try writing something?*
> —James Tate, *"Teaching the Ape to Write Poems"*

I've spent my whole life searching for magic: overcame
my pounding heart in order to lift my astral foot above my head
and correctly guess the queen of hearts which my ex-wife said
she always held above her head; focused all my force of mind
so I could rattle a teacup in its saucer when I could've
    done it with my foot.

But I cherish those meditations, even when I fell asleep,
those long involved fallings inward and levitations upward
to see what Sis' was up to though I could've used the phone.

But I found if you stare a fact in the face down to its fractals
the real can be intuited; and even though sometimes you'll miss
the obvious and maybe get embarrassed, it still feels magical.

Have I come full circle just to say in the mist of a "senior
    moment,"
Now what was it I was looking for? Am I the prodigal fish
    who went off
to spend the rest of his life searching for the magical thing
    called water?

But when your knees lock up looking for some change
    you dropped
and you find your long-lost glasses, it makes the ordinary
    seem miraculous.
Maybe I could've hopped another life and arrived where I
    already am,

but there's something I can't quite remember, like a post-it note
stuck on a fridge in another life, that says "You're special"
though it might've said "Get pickles." But even mistakes
    are mystical.

Like all the adepts have said for ages, it's the getting what
    I've got
and the getting where I am that makes real life feel magical.

Star Trek

There are three hundred trillion stars
for each man, woman, and child on earth.
It seems God made just enough for me to wish on.
But not enough to stop me from worrying about death.

So I practiced how I'd be immortal,
picturing eons of blue light years
in which I let light take over for me being the emergency.
But it only slowed down whatever I shot past.

Then I stopped at a traffic light
where a blind woman in a crosswalk gave me the look
that said *Hey, I'm trying to get across.*
We'll all be less than light soon enough.

So now I'm working on the opposite of what a black hole is,
being in the here-and-now so totally that I'm everywhere
    at once.
I'm cleansing the Golden Flower of Clouded Consciousness,
training my breath to break my mind's obsessive speech. But
the hardest part will be trying to stop smoking first.

Parable of the Burden

When I was little I loved to be good,
and loved to be of use to whoever could use me.

I held the world's record
for the fastest errands in my family
and only the most suicidal grains of mica
would dare to flash when I swept.

He's good, so good, my parents would whisper
as if I were a mark with an overflowing wallet.
Each day for me was a cargo of goods
I had to send sailing out of sight.

That's when I decided to be "difficult,"
when everyone who loved me then
died waiting for me to grow up.

Who wouldn't be good, I thought,
if pleasing others could ease the burden
of being good, if like those great transcendent souls,
or like me when I was little, I could've lifted those burdens
like a toast to and from myself.

Routine

Just before my father
entered emptiness,
when I finally screwed up
the courage to ask him
what he thought was wrong with me,
he said, *Tell me the truth,
have I been a good father?*
And to make him feel better I just laughed.

My son has a question
he's flown 2,000 miles
through snow-laden clouds
to ask. But all we do is joke around,
like me and my father,
like a couple of morticians over a corpse

who hope that whatever life force
and love this person had
are safe somewhere
even if it's only in each other
as we turn off the lights
and go back into the world
with the knowledge
of how delicate we are
and with such great care
we can only laugh.

Heaven

Sometimes I can feel mother and father watching me,
giggling at their tadpole squiggling toward the after-life,
who's taking a lifetime to get over a few old embarrassments,
like living your life while not being yourself.

But nowadays I know I'm real
and that I'm where all longings long to be,
and that my parents up there,
like me when I was a kid,
are longing for all eternity
to be something as astonishing as themselves.

Their old explosions over spilled milk
now seem to them as impossible and majestic
as Moses parting the Red Sea,
and the sun up there, which is just a shadowy pinprick of light
so infinite it's been rarified into spirit,
is burning away in its glory, fueled by making
its gazillion mistakes a minute.

Living Large

Sometimes I feel like
I'm living inside a period
at the end of a sentence
I'm not privy to,
and it doesn't come close
to meaning what I'd meant
though I admit I like the feeling
of how stopping everything makes me seem
larger than what I'd meant.

My daughter would always start her sentences
with *First a ball*, and then we'd laugh,
picturing her dribbling a bright yellow ball
that'd end with so *what are we going to do?*

And I didn't want to say, as some urge of hers
unrolled its windswept tangle of language,
Darling, we're doing it,
since what she said was better than what she meant,
which must've come from our lectures
to her that basically said we're bigger than you.

I'd like to think my daughter was performing
a *double entendre* when she said to me, *Farther,
In the beginning was the ball,* inside of which,
swirling with understanding, collapsing and expanding,
she was my grand potential.

But in terms of the cosmic clock
and given the fact they've discovered after our heart's stopped
and we're pronounced clinically brain-dead,
that something's still thinking our thoughts, it makes me realize
the glory of being the last in a long line of followers

whose job is just to say *I'm here. You're not alone.* Period.

Not that I can see where I'm going, which is a gift
I overlooked and thus am overwhelmed by,
but dear daughter, like you, *first a ball,* is a power
that makes me feel I've flung the window open
like an exclamation point, which makes me feel
larger than what I'd meant.

The "I Used To Be (Blank) But Now I Am (Blank) Exercise"

The "I Used To Be (Blank) But Now I Am (Blank) Exercise"
seemed like a great idea
for examining the changes in his life.

But, day after day, he could think of nothing
to fill in the blanks
except the nothing that followed his thinking.

Each day, disgusted with its blankness,
he balled each sheet of paper up
and threw it away
so that he wouldn't have to be
the one with nothing on it. And that
made his mind feel fresh again. It was the paper,
blinded by nothingness, crumpled by failure,
that carried all this

into oblivion. Isn't that what oblivion was
made of? What more profound lesson
about oblivion could there be than not being able
to come up with something? Nothing!

Thus it was that he was inspired to write
to the part of himself he lost on blank paper.
It would start with the old address, "O Blivious…!"
He liked the idea of the "I Used To Be (Blank)
But Now I Am (Blank) Exercise"
and was pleased with his results.

Writing on Not Writing

I can feel my ship about to come in.
A white ship in a snowstorm moving in.

The ship is made of gulls
huddled together in the shape of a ship.

When it arrives, they will fly out into the storm,
leaving a space inside it clear as reason.

I can tell there's going to be a blizzard
of being somewhere else any minute

because the noise of time eating itself up
is the noise of listening
that looks like a seething, florid whiteout of wings

While Reading the Work of Another Poet,

a moving van arrives inside me
with a cargo of dark urges.

Suddenly I've got 16 wheels
and a mouth full of diesel
and the whole world
has dragged its stuff to the curb.

Woodpecker Event Horizon

This morning I'm listening to my slow-motion recording
of a woodpecker knocking its brains out
so I can study, blow-by-blow, the decisions it makes
as it bangs its head through a tree and calls it home.

Because I've lived my life by studying
how I've lived my life, bobsledding
through my tunnel vision into a suicidal white-out
that'll return me to living
in the split-second stillness between blows
when I lift my bald-crested head and zap into full Zen mode.

I believe your mind's not in your brain
but continually flares from your entire body,
like when you sense someone across a crowded room
is concentrating on you and you turn and nail who's doing it.
I call that unconscious moment the "lacuna of lucidity."
Whoa, see that!? As I said it I wondered why I sound
so Germanic whenever I'm grasping myself.
I'm talking about that sweet zone between blows
where I don't know what I'm doing, but my doing knows.

The Rest of Me

What I remember about my near-death experience
is trying to steel-jacket myself with happiness,
just in case I died and woke up atomized on the other side,
I could, as Ma used to yell, at least try to look grateful.

Time slowed down so I could look back at the many lives
    I've led
the way kids stare at tropical fish, and, I rolled around inside
the feeling of being alive, thinking this tiny whine should
    be equal
to the task of carrying anything that might be left of me.

And I woke, feeling like I'd won a bet when the fix was in.
Except now the weird thing is when I'm commuting,
and the drivers passing me look locked inside a life
where Getting There is all there is, I think maybe I left a
    part of me

on the other side, since I could beam myself over and
    whisper in their ear
the Buddhist blessing "Live as if you were dead," and then
    look back at
myself feeling finally I'm living the secret life I never lived.

The Failed Calligrapher

I am the failed calligrapher
many come to see
when they feel like
saying something beautifully.

The art is in trying
to capture what things are
as they graze on what they stand for.

Many will come to you
the Master said
change change
this is the work

you must be
for all of them
everything
or you will only copy
what you see.

Not the Work, Not the Life

The work mattered
in the way I get involved
in the wanderings of an ant.

And the life mattered too
though it's too late for the life I've led,
like the regret I feel
after wiping an ant off my shoe.

But the hand in yours, a word and wink,
all the criss-crossings in the impossible fabric
of being here, what vault can hold that?

I snuggle into this impasse like an axe
in the chest of a paradox, like mother screaming
Supper's getting cold! meaning she was getting old
and incapable of being wise or simple
and just too complicated to flower.

Sweet Dreams

No matter how rocky our day,
our dreams will easily absorb us.

You place my hand on your breast
like a book mark, as if to say

This is where we left off,
as if saying nothing about this

is enough to pour us spooning like twin moons
over the edge of a volatile abyss inside the earth.

We start out with my hand on your breast
as if to say whatever miraculous thing may happen to us
we know what's best.

How Do You like my Hair?

Shampooing her hair,
my wife explains the universe
is just a bubble floating in a foaming mass of other bubbles
while God's mind is everywhere at once.

This, she says while rinsing it clean,
accounts for all the little blips we experience
like mental telepathy and transubstantiation.
Do you believe in ghosts? she asks

while blow-drying her matted hair
into auburn cotton candy.
Yes, I say, and bend down and stare godlike
at a bubble left shining on the drain's steel rim
where my wife and I are reflected talking on it, talking,
before it slips soundlessly over the abyss.

So how do you like my hair?

Ashville

He made furniture
from exotic woods
that intrigued him,

like the Arabian ottoman
from purple African wood
in honor of a girl he loved as a kid
who smelled like amethyst
as if she had washed herself in wishes.

He liked the idea
that people could relax
inside
whatever he was making.

Then one day the doctor said
in a month you'll be dead.

Never making another chair
was the way he'd always felt anyway,
as if something were missing,
like his place in life,
a feeling that only the making
of another chair
could replace.

The Wisdom of the Idiots

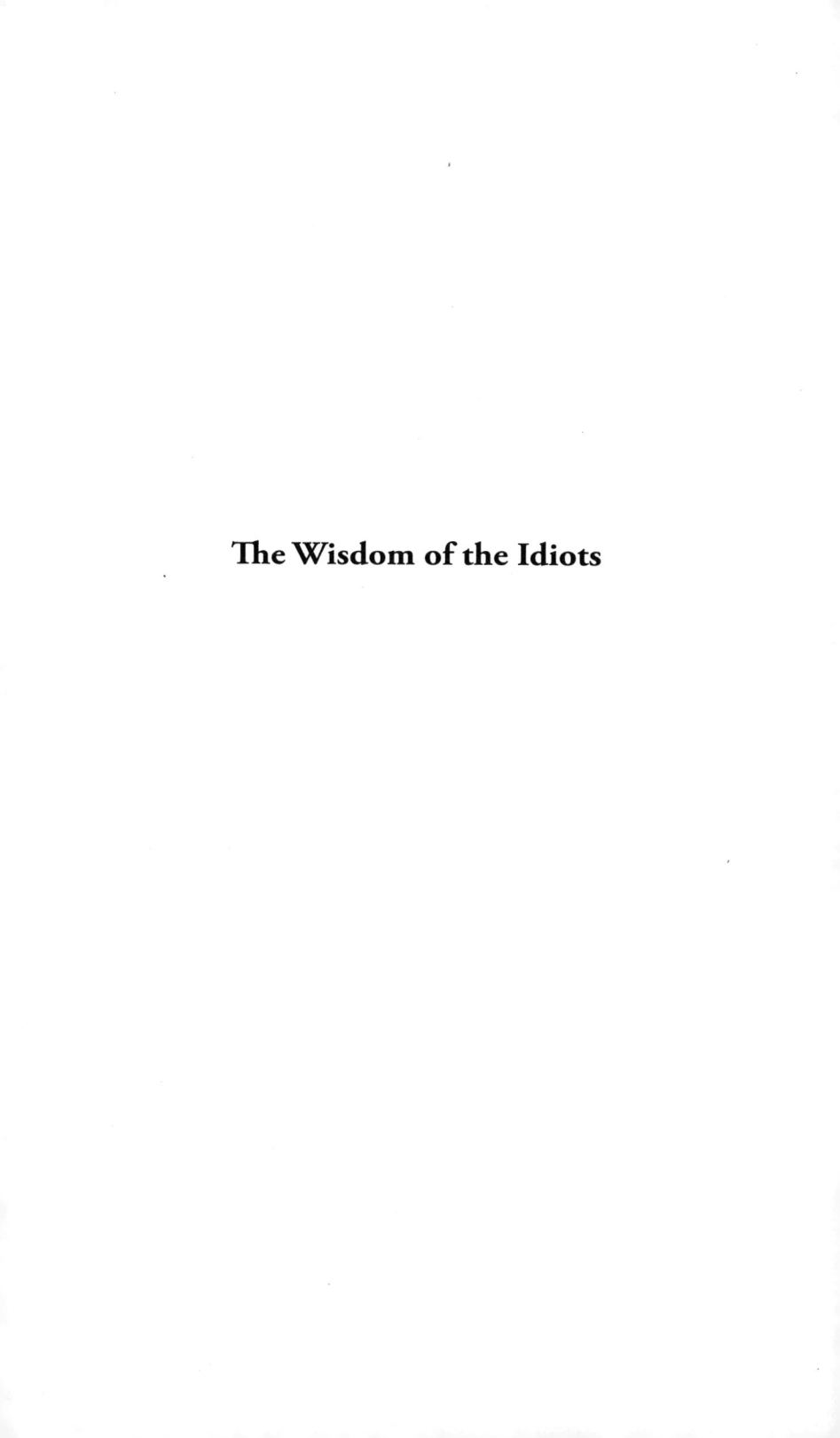

Indebted

Thirty years ago
someone stole a book from my car
and left me a ratty old-lady's purple snap purse
with a single penny inside it.

After thirty years of feeling ripped off,
tonight it finally occurred to me—That's all she had!
A penny, which in her mind wasn't nearly enough.
So she left me her purse.

Unless

Each moment is a thirst-quenching well.
But not this one. This one is poisoned
with hope and distractions.

It needs a songbird and some incense, please,
something to inspire it.

Unless it just happens.
Unless the moment is what it is.
Unless, unless, say it again, un-less.

When I Heard My Name Being Called

I walked outside.
But everything looked
just like I left it.

When I heard my name being called
I went inside. But there were the usual
horses of want riding the roads of need.

I think what I heard
like the feeling of leaving
without saying goodbye
was the body of completion
trying to arrive.

Perhaps following that feeling
has been my gift, like the bread crumbs
others have dropped
that have allowed me to hear my name.

Blue Skies

Thich Nhat Hanh says
insight is always there
like a clear blue sky.

Its pleasure is to feel
it has just been born,
ours, that we have just given birth.

Like when father use to yell at me
Stop walking backward!
mother would say he's not walking backward,
he's backward-walking.

Whatever You Do

It is said the difference between
an adept and a child
lighting a candle
is that one acts as if he has
never seen the power fire has
to return anything it touches to light
while the other seems transfixed
as if something beautiful
were being illuminated inside him.

It did not say which was which.

Vacancy

If you want to make a difference
go to an empty place,

fill it up with yourself
and then let go of that and wait
until the place is empty again.

If you bring all of you with you,
what you leave with will make an enormous difference.

Mindfulness

The vase that confuses
the feeling of water
filling it up
with the water
filling it up
is no longer a vase.

But the vase that remains
a vase while feeling like water
filling it up
is also a flower.

On Purpose

How victoriously the iron nail resists
the converging wills of wind and wood.

As perfectly as its corruption completes
its resistance to what it is.

The Deep Blue Sea of Surrender

When the fisherman who wouldn't let go
hooked the fish who wouldn't get caught,

who each one thought he was and wasn't
was the line about to snap.

They feared they'd tear themselves apart
though each lived inside the illusion

of who was fishing and who was caught.

And then the line between them snapped.
But not the illusion of what each one thought he lost.

The Iridescent Flashings of The Integral One

The acid pages of my book on consciousness
are eating their way back to the land
of sun and wind and rain they came from.

Page 28, thin as this moment's edge,
is giving way to Lao Tsu 2,000 years ago

who's explaining how things are always becoming
what they were while remaining what they are.

The Wisdom of the Idiots

They hear the rain inside of silence
and the silence inside of rain.
Wetness and dryness are the same

difference
between what things are
and the names we have for them.

But each thing
in and of itself
is the only name it contains.

This is what people who have held themselves open
all their lives attain,
the old ones who delight and annoy us
and remind us of children.

Curriculum Vitae

Like a bird with a chest full of medals,
hardly able to walk, the vain live under a day-glo sky
dyed by what they believe they have accomplished.

Isn't it ironic that only the most beautiful birds,
like peacocks and parrots, birds that have colored themselves
with their desire to be seen, can only make an ugly squawk
or repeat what they've heard. They do not hear

how everywhere else the drab birds of the workaday world
are ribboning the trees with improvised song,
their delight their only philosophy.

Hanging Branches

on a photograph by David Akiba

Winter branches reflected on a lake
        reach across the sky.

It is its own self-portrait,
        light's shadow on water speaking to the dark.

Where the branches dip their tips
      into their reflection, sipping on what they will become,

there's a single ripple crossing the lake that stands for
      everything.

Inside Out

I carried a sense of myself,
like a bubble in a carpenter's level,
assuming wherever I went
would lead to water and then
I'd be balanced, leveled, and centered,
a web of human breath
floating on teeming change
without any fixed center
either in myself or in what I was
measuring myself against,
until I remembered the magnitudes of scale
and the permutations of change
are infinite and everlasting
and that, by definition,
anywhere in the infinite is its center.

Catching the Hummingbird

It's lush here tonight.
Everything I planted last year
thrived on my distraction.

Now I'd like to plant something quiet
above the commotion of wild grasses
to attract the mythic hummingbird,
some tufts of green Not-Doing,
the blue flower of What Blossoms Beyond Waiting,
the golden-throated trumpet flowers of Sitting Still
so I can sneak up on it, catch a glimpse of it,
then prune my glimpsing from the glimpse.

Pouring Water Downhill

Before the spark that I am goes out
in the larger darkness, I smile down

on my children who at their age are entangled
in greed and ambition and jealousy
because my heart is light.

It's slowly giving away like the moon's soft light
what has always been freely borrowed.

Why should I settle their accounts for them
when my own have led me here?

Because I have come to see they were my treasure,
I will have a note sent to each after I'm dead
saying *You were my favorite.*

Let them, like me, be water pouring downhill,
smashing into obstacle after obstacle,
find the most carefree way.

Unconditional Surrender

The Flicker

This is in honor of the flicker
that sings its heart out on my roof everyday
though no other flicker comes.

If I can't be sure of the language of joy
can I at least know something that is?

There is a flicker flapping its wings and playing
with the name of whatever it's doing.

The tiny bit of him that weighs something
is holding down the house

while the larger part of him that weighs nothing
lifts it up.

Now

Wouldn't it be horrible to live life backwards,
be born old with all your wisdom and faith,
knowledge and achievements,
gradually sinking like the Himalayas back into liquid?

Each day in the bazaar, the heart, lost in the swirl
of its entourage and finery, bypasses the soul
hidden behind her black *chador.*

He thinks he can create *déjà vu* by force.
And the soul, poor thing, being everywhere at once,
doesn't know backwards from forwards.

Doorway

> *What you depart from is not the way.*
> —Ezra Pound

When I was awake and aware
I could place my hand under a bird
from a great distance
and make it hop its life-weight.

I could rip away the air
between things and their colors
so that I became what I saw
and saw what I was in everything.

But how I got there and ended up here
in an everyday life is a mystery.
Maybe someone's hand was under me.

It's the same mystery as how the image of a door
has just occurred to me and then the thought
that neither side of a door knows what's on the other side
except whenever it's opened, and how if it stayed open
it would no longer be a door.

The Tao of Light

When I learned that black radiation
is an invisible light emitted
by a hot solid like the human body,
which is a perfect absorber of light,

I realized how I've lived in the shadow
of whatever I didn't see,
and that the light I cast made shadows
out of wherever I happened to be.

So when The Bible says God separated light from darkness,
meaning darkness isn't the absence of light,
the answer to the question "What is the opposite of light?"
turns out to depend on who's doing the talking
and who they're talking to.

Continuity Drives Through the Division of Things

I've learned to connect by letting go,
soaring out of myself into the fullness
of everything I've ignored.

Right now the sound of roaring lawnmowers
gnawing across this subdivision
shimmers as deliciously as my pool.

When they built it and painted its insides white,
I asked, how will the water become blue?
They said just fill it up and the sky will do the rest.

Prescience

> *The entire image of a destiny is packed into a tiny acorn,*
> *the seed of a huge oak on small shoulders.*
> —James Hillman, *The Soul's Code*

I go outside at 4 a.m.
There's the glow of morning but it's night.
Night-morning, I like this very much,
the feeling of silver shining through tarnish.

When dawn comes I go inside to write about this,
leave the constellations of buzzing insects like crazed pins
to make sure the light doesn't slip.

I think, nothing can help me with this work.
Nothing can help me with this work.

Me

My ego likes to think of himself
in charge of me,
but he's only a star-spangled mouse
in a tiny cork boat
being blown over parfait seas,
lost in the fog of whatever he thinks,
wherever he happens to be.

He doesn't know the sea he's floating on
is floating on other seas,
or that his reflection ripped apart by wind and waves
can never be lost and can't be drowned
because it lives inside something larger
inside of me that is immortal.
And yet look how pathetically he looks up to me.

Who, What, When, Where, and Why

I walk out under the blue sky
of my own being
that I call here.

What happens next
I call change.

If I climb out of myself, put my hands on my hips
and look around like I'm in charge,
it's time to enlarge my heart,

to see again like a thing without eyes,
like the growth rings of tree
whose single eye inside rises fifty feet high.

Incarnation

A friend of mine won't eat pork because pigs are so intelligent.
Another won't eat anything smarter than an egg.
And still another won't eat food that had a face.

But I've seen gnats fall in love with other gnats across a
 crowded room.
Seen a single seed, over time, lift a ton of wood above its head.
And don't some of my best ideas come from meditating
 on rocks?

So, please, whoever has the true and secret knowledge, tell
 us what to eat.

Remind us, when we lift our knife and fork in praise of
 our transcendence
over everything beneath us, that there are forces that can
 crystallize mist
into exquisite works of ice that love melting back to mist again.

Remind us, before we eat, that we are monumental,
momentary works of mist. And that everyone and everything
that ever existed has brought us here.

The New Gods

*I imagine the gods saying, we will
make it up to you.*
—Jack Gilbert

Because we no longer believe,
the old gods are rising from rivers
and woods and volcanoes and rocks
and the greater darkness and the notion of love
and the carcasses of beasts.

They are dissipating in vapors
of outdated ecstasy and awe and archaic dread
and prophetic visions and ratchetings of catechism
and telemetry and polemics and blanked-out paroxysm,

hoisting us into the cosmic sea broth
we first burst from as a one-celled,
blind, and wild-eyed pulsation
for ten pair of shoes and a vacation in Miami

as if the image of us in the mirror could feel
the godhead flying through us in the tonnage of urge
that makes the universe expand and us
drag this willful life we leave to plant our little flag

on the airless moon of the soul and scour it for a rock,
a drop of water, some microscopic fossil of another life,
another us beyond us from which the inner life has dropped us.

Live As If You Were Dead

Everything effervesces with change,
even remembering who you are and
by what secret vow of allegiance you came.

This is the place where I get stuck.
The stone. The seed. The Throne.

I need to return everything I've collected and buried
in photographs and poems back to the living.

Live as if I were a typical little old lady.

Track Record

> *My exile's search for cure is just more illness*
> —Mutran Khalil Mutran

My Wise Old Man and Inner Child,
who have no use for sex or getting liquored-up,
spend their time in the jade-green shade
of the pavilion to oblivion
keeping me steady
by rolling up the passage of time
which is the path I am between them
into a profane scroll of transgressions
I will sing from during my coming
eonic blackout between this life and the next one,
until, light as chance, easy as grace,
I'll be buoyed by a humility
that knows I'm just your average Joe
arguing about the reality of oblivion
with some other 7-billion-to-1 long shot
that just came in.

Unconditional Surrender

Though we've been unable to remember
even a single moment we swirled in
before our birth,

there is a lagoon each moment floats on
in the suspended gravity of the soul's perfume
that connects our exile to infinity and the spirit to eternity.

When you dive in, it remembers who you are
as completely as anesthesia can forget the flattened life
that opens onto this one.

It has nothing to do with remembering,
except remembering you have the strength to break
and ride this lion of surrender.

Fragments

Remember when you were little
and could shout like the yellow sun
on the horizon *Here I Come!*,
before your self-image was a light bulb
in the fridge of your self-esteem
and you weren't afraid of anything in life
because there wasn't any difference
between everything in life and you?
Remember how large you felt?

*

When I find myself wanting to be famous
for what little talent I possess,
I compose the best poem I can
on two halves of a potato in my head.

You Will Live a Very Long Time…*in bed*

The old ones add an extra goodbye
the way we used to add the phrase *in bed*
to the end of whatever our fortune cookies said:
You will achieve great wisdom…*in bed*.

They float beneath glassy swells of beta waves
like talking heads worrying whether there'll be an afterlife
or how someone will get their body down three flights of stairs
after they're dead.

One says, *It's like falling out of a plane,*
you can't plan for it on the way down.
Another says, *but with luck, God willing,*
maybe we'll land face up.

All the Power That Has Ever Existed Is Here Now

How the Mountain, being made to ponder the flowing mind
of sand and wind and fire and water, is being made
every second of its existence, to slowly give in.

How a single-cell animal honors splitting into two
because the fear of disappearing forever is equal to
the promise that nothing ever will.

How a sperm cell poking its head inside a yellow sun
somehow knows it has become what it always knew it would
before it ever could have known it could.

Take me, I'm disappearing too, while trying to stay in shape.
But my body's sole desire is to drift and mate forever and ever
with the formlessness of change that contains it.

Sea Level

The great white swans
gliding on their black shadows
dream at night of black feet paddling furiously.

*

Wonder and desire are how the self changes
into the camouflage of everything.

*

When Buddha was becoming Buddha,
evolving from rock to tree to fish,
he didn't worry "What if I can't find the way back?"

*

On my way back down,
I remember to nod to the rocks
on their journey to be us.

*

Now, if a lion were to charge me,
I would change into water
as when a child I changed the foaming breakers
into legions of lions.

*

Even if I admitted it's all been a mistake,
I would not start over.
My children are more beautiful than me.

Jack Myers was the 2003-2004 Texas Poet Laureate, and he is the author/editor of seventeen books of and about poetry. He has taught creative writing at Southern Methodist Univeristy since 1975 and is a former member of the faculty at Vermont College's graduate writing program. His work has received the Violet Crown Award from the Writers League of Texas, fellowships from The National Endowment for the Arts, and awards from The Texas Institute of Letters. He has four children and lives with his wife, Thea Temple, who is Executive Director of The Writer's Garret, in Mesquite, Texas.